THE Animal Cartoon BOOK

Robert Ainsworth

SCHOLASTIC INC.
New York   Toronto   London   Auckland   Sydney
Mexico City   New Delhi   Hong Kong

DEDICATED TO ALL THE FASCINATING ANIMALS OF
THE WORLD.
LIFE WOULDN'T BE HALF AS INTERESTING
WITHOUT YOU!

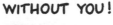

ISBN 0-439-10845-4

12 11 10 9 8   5 6 7 8 9/0

Printed in the U.S.A.   08

First Scholastic printing, September 1999

Typeset in Tekton

CONTENTS

About this book	4
How to use this book	5
Face shapes	6–7
Faces step-by-step	8–11
Bears and dogs	12–13
Face shapes—rabbit	14
Face features	15
Faces—domestic animals	16–17
Faces—woodland animals	18
Faces—Australian animals	19
Faces—African animals	20–21
Faces—big cats	22–23
Faces—apes	24
Faces—wild dogs	25
Faces—domestic dogs	26–27
Faces—N American animals	28–29
Faces—S American animals	30
Faces—Asian animals	31
Faces—European animals	32–33
Faces—Polar region animals	34
Faces—domestic birds	35
Faces—wild birds	36–37
Faces—reptiles	38
Faces—water animals	39
Bodies of animals	40–43
'Cartoonish' style hints	44–45
'Cartoon' features	46–47
Expression in faces	48–49
Shapes in bodies	50
Funny bodies	51
Cute upright bodies	52–54
More cute animals	55
Dorky animals	56–57
Animal jokes	58–59
Animal riddles	60
Lettering for cartoons	61
Index	62–63

I LIKE THESE CONTENTS!

LEAVE SOME FOR ME!

ABOUT this BOOK

When I was young I wished there was a simple drawing manual—a book that would help me draw animals quickly and easily.

Often when I tried to draw a horse, for instance, it turned out looking more like a dog—or worse still, it didn't look like any known animal at all!

That's why I've written this book: to help you develop your drawing skills, easily.

As I was writing it I tried to remember what I wanted to know when I was learning to draw. I hope you like it and find it useful.

HAVE FUN!

Robert Ainsworth

HOLD TIGHT!

Gidday!

So... to make it easy, just look for the **SHAPES**

HERE ARE MOST OF THE SHAPES YOU WILL FIND:

CIRCLE OVAL SQUARE RECTANGLE TRIANGE HEART PEANUT DIAMOND HALF-CIRCLE SAUSAGE TEAR-DROP GUITAR

SOME ANIMAL FACE SHAPES

A PEANUT FOR A PEANUT...?

WANT ME TO PLAY YOU A TUNE?

EVEN *PEOPLE* HAVE DIFFERENT SHAPED FACES AND FEATURES

BOO! HOO! I'VE GOT A SAUSAGE FOR A MOUTH!

REMEMBER:

ALMOST ALL THINGS ARE EASY TO DRAW, WHEN YOU THINK OF THEM AS SHAPES THAT HAVE BEEN 'FLESHED-OUT.'

LOOK at THIS!

THIS IS SO SIMPLE IT'S NOT FUNNY!!

ANYONE can draw animal faces by using the following method.

Just follow the steps:

①
Draw a diamond.

NOSE

②
Draw 2 circles touching the 2 top sides of the diamond.

2 EYEBALLS

③
Draw 2 circles touching the 2 bottom sides of the diamond.

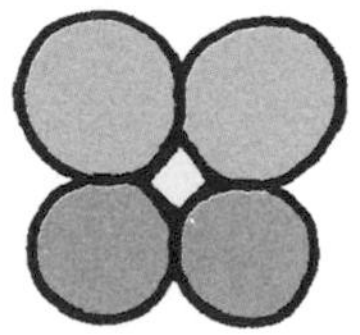

2 CHEEKS

HAHA
HAHA

8

NOW...

basically all we've got left to draw is a **HEAD**, **EARS** and **MOUTH**,

SO... **LET'S FINISH IT OFF.**

But what will we make it? I know...

a *MOUSE*!!

---

④ Draw a big circle around everything you've drawn so far.

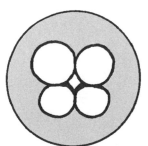

HEAD

⑤ Draw 2 circles in the top 'corners' of the biggest circle.

EARS

⑥ Draw a half-circle under the cheeks.

MOUTH

TURN OVER TO FINISH IT...

Now that we've drawn all of the basic shapes, we can **bring it to LIFE!**

⑦ Draw 2 rectangles under the cheeks, in the mouth.

TEETH

⑧
- Add two dots for the eyes.
- Fill in the inside of the mouth.
- Draw lines for whiskers — and dots for whisker holes...

EYE-DOTS, WHISKERS, INSIDE OF MOUTH

⑨ ... and finally
- Darken the 2 bottom sides of the diamond (for the nose-holes).
- Darken inside the ears (for the ear-holes).

SQUEEK!

NOSE & EAR HOLES

YOU CAN DRAW ALL OF THE ANIMALS ON THE NEXT PAGE THIS SAME WAY.

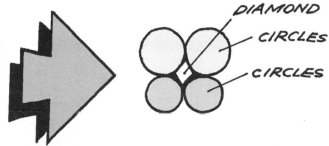

Notice how all of these animal faces start with the same basic shapes.

DIAMOND
CIRCLES
CIRCLES

The only major things you need to change for each animal are the shape of the head, ears and mouth.

- YOU CAN TRY A VARIETY OF SHAPES FOR THE PUPILS IN THE EYES, TOO.
- OF COURSE, THE MEAT-EATING ANIMALS HAVE SHARP TEETH, AND THE VEGETABLE-EATING ANIMALS HAVE BIG, BLUNT TEETH.

Grizzle, Grizzle!

woof! woof!

Animals such as Bears and Dogs

(which have long snouts)

can be drawn slightly differently...

like this...

**NOSE
TRIANGLE**

**CHEEK
CIRCLES**

**SNOUT
CIRCLE**

HEAD CIRCLE

EYEBALLS

EYE DOTS

MOUTH

EARS

*SNIFF
SNIFF*

WHISKERS

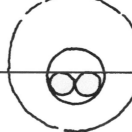
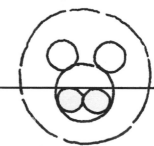

BEARS

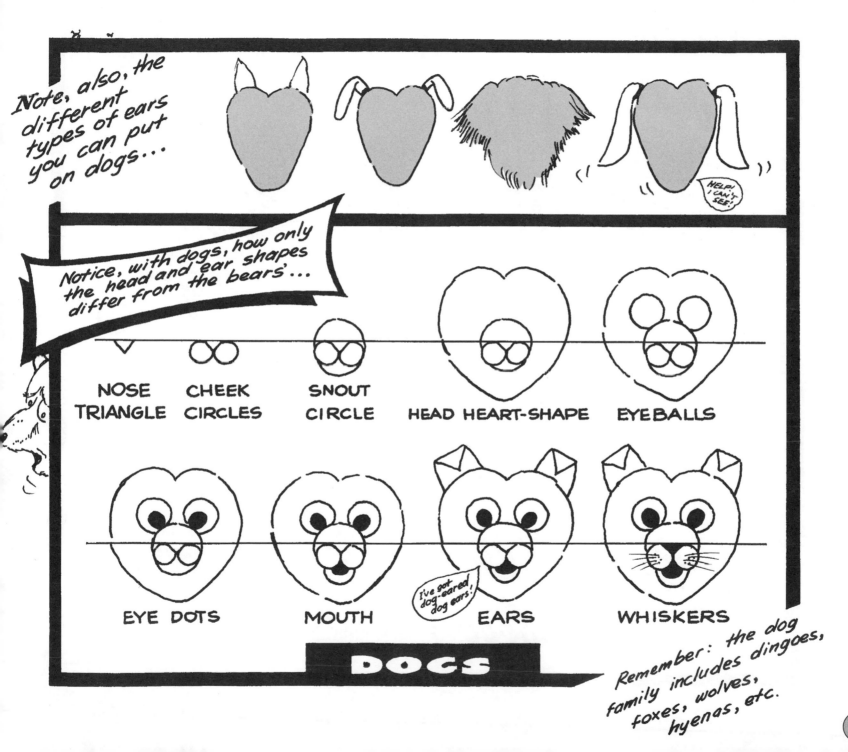

Note, also, the different types of ears you can put on dogs...

HELP! I CAN'T SEE!

Notice, with dogs, how only the head and ear shapes differ from the bears'...

NOSE TRIANGLE

CHEEK CIRCLES

SNOUT CIRCLE

HEAD HEART-SHAPE

EYEBALLS

EYE DOTS

MOUTH

I've got dog-eared dog ears!

EARS

WHISKERS

DOGS

Remember: the dog family includes dingoes, foxes, wolves, hyenas, etc.

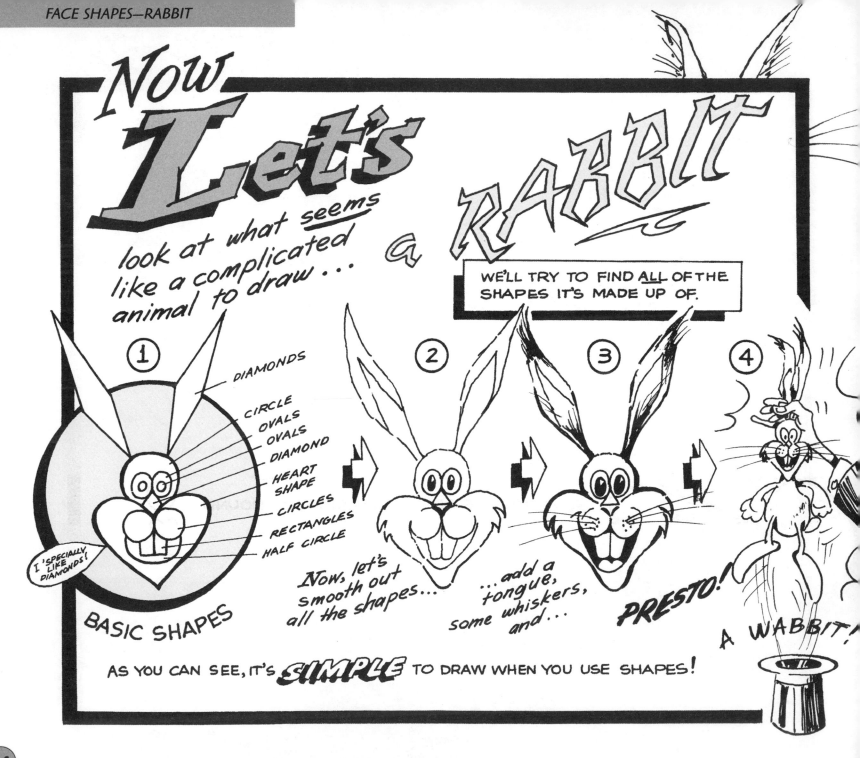

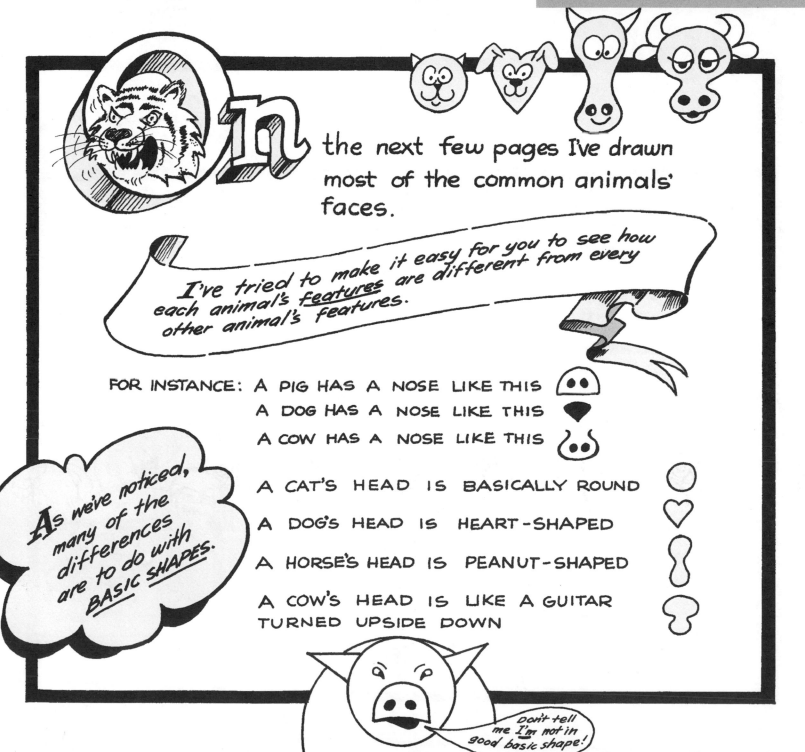

On the next few pages I've drawn most of the common animals' faces.

I've tried to make it easy for you to see how each animal's <u>features</u> are different from every other animal's features.

As we've noticed, many of the differences are to do with <u>BASIC SHAPES.</u>

FOR INSTANCE: A PIG HAS A NOSE LIKE THIS

A DOG HAS A NOSE LIKE THIS

A COW HAS A NOSE LIKE THIS

A CAT'S HEAD IS BASICALLY ROUND

A DOG'S HEAD IS HEART-SHAPED

A HORSE'S HEAD IS PEANUT-SHAPED

A COW'S HEAD IS LIKE A GUITAR TURNED UPSIDE DOWN

Don't tell me I'm not in good basic shape!

ANIMAL Faces Domestic Animals

Take note of the basic shapes of each animal's features: head shape, ears, nose, mouth, eyes, etc — and notice how they differ from each other animal's features.

	CAT	DOG	HORSE	COW
BASIC SHAPES	CIRCLE FOR HEAD	HEART SHAPE FOR HEAD	PEANUT SHAPE FOR HEAD	GUITAR SHAPE FOR HEAD
FRONT VIEW	MEOW!	WOOF!	MOO!	HEY! THAT'S MY LINE!
SIDE VIEW				

MAIN HEAD SHAPE →

16

BIG CAT
Faces
TIGER
LION
LEOPARD
PANTHER
BASIC SHAPES
FRONT VIEW
SIDE VIEW
HOW DID THE LEOPARD GET HIS SPOTS?
IT'S ALL DONE WITH COMPUTER GRAPHICS.
SCRATCH MY BACK, AND I'LL SCRATCH YOURS...

APE Faces

HOOT! HOOT!

	MONKEY	CHIMPANZEE	GORILLA	BABOON
BASIC SHAPES				
FRONT VIEW				
SIDE VIEW				

HI, BROTHER!

WHAT A NUT!

24

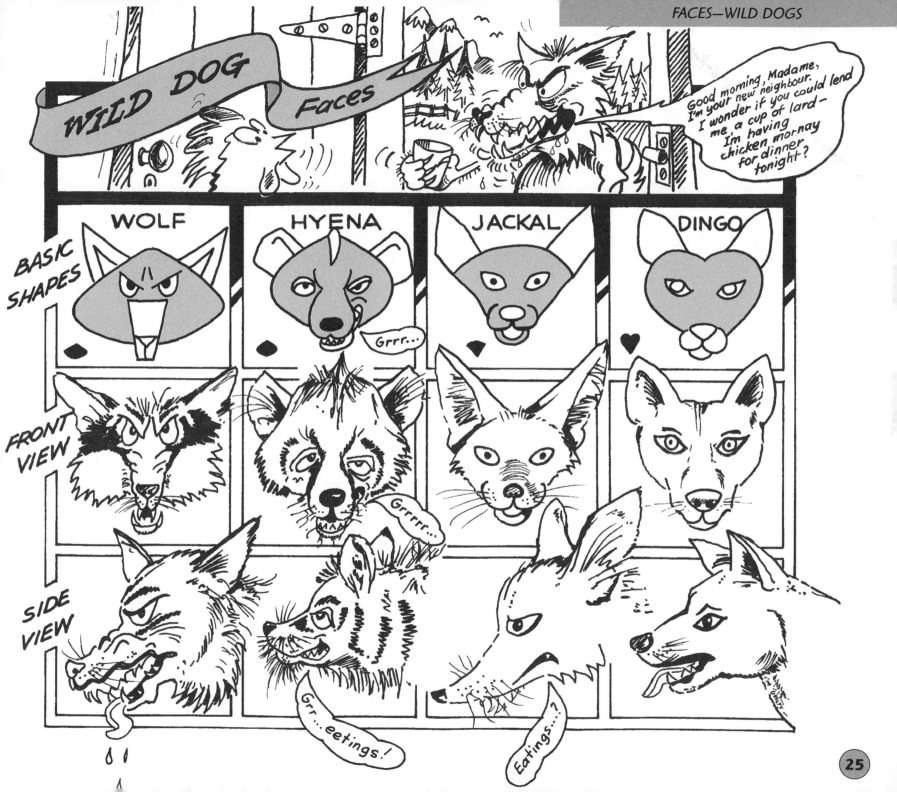

North American Large Animal FACES

BEAR BISON DEER MOOSE

BASIC SHAPES

FRONT VIEW

SIDE VIEW

THE REIN IN SPAIN STAYS MAINLY IN THE PLAIN...

DEER ME, WHAT A PAIN!

MOO, HOO!

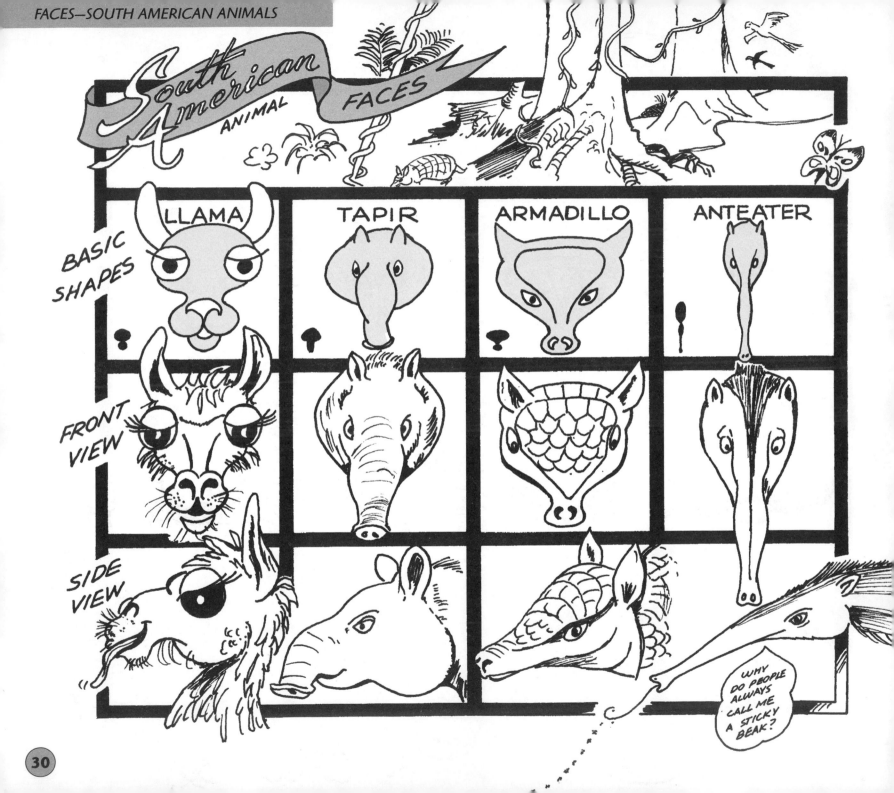

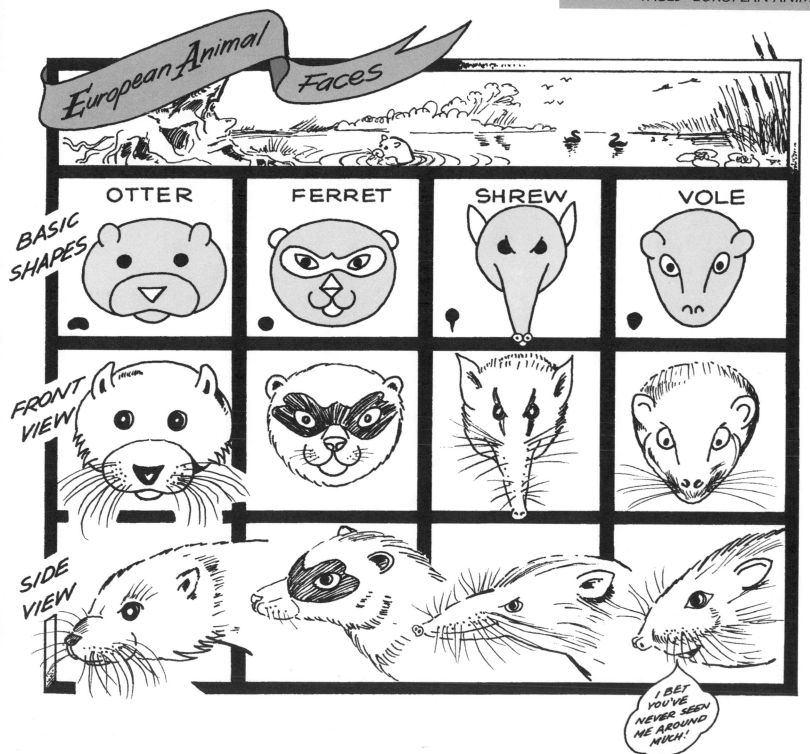

POLAR REGION ANIMAL Faces

	SEAL	WALRUS	PENGUIN	POLAR BEAR
BASIC SHAPES				
FRONT VIEW				
SIDE VIEW				

I'VE GOT TO THE BACK TO THE WALL, RUS.

A LITTLE TO THE LEFT... THAT'S IT, WALLY.

COOL IT, MAN!

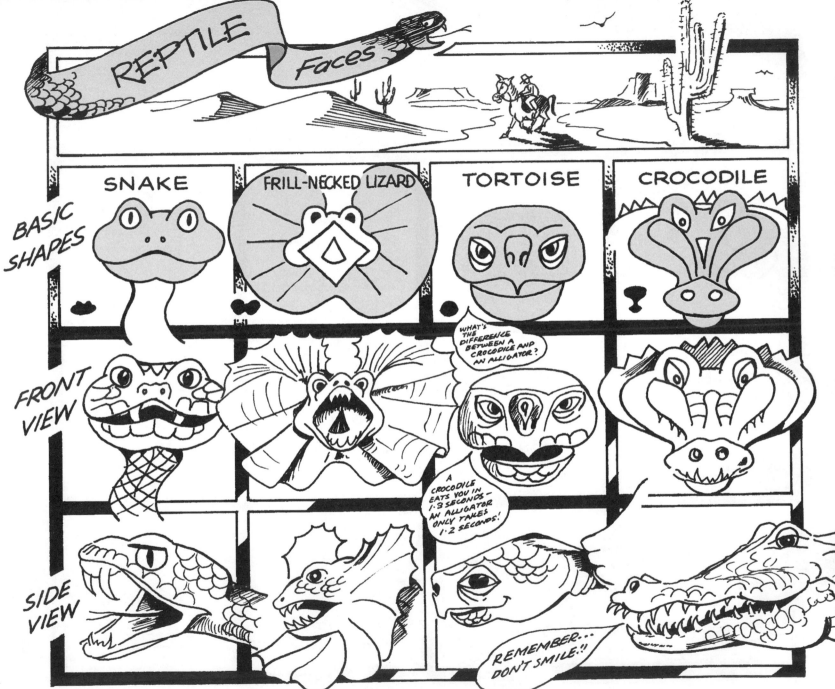

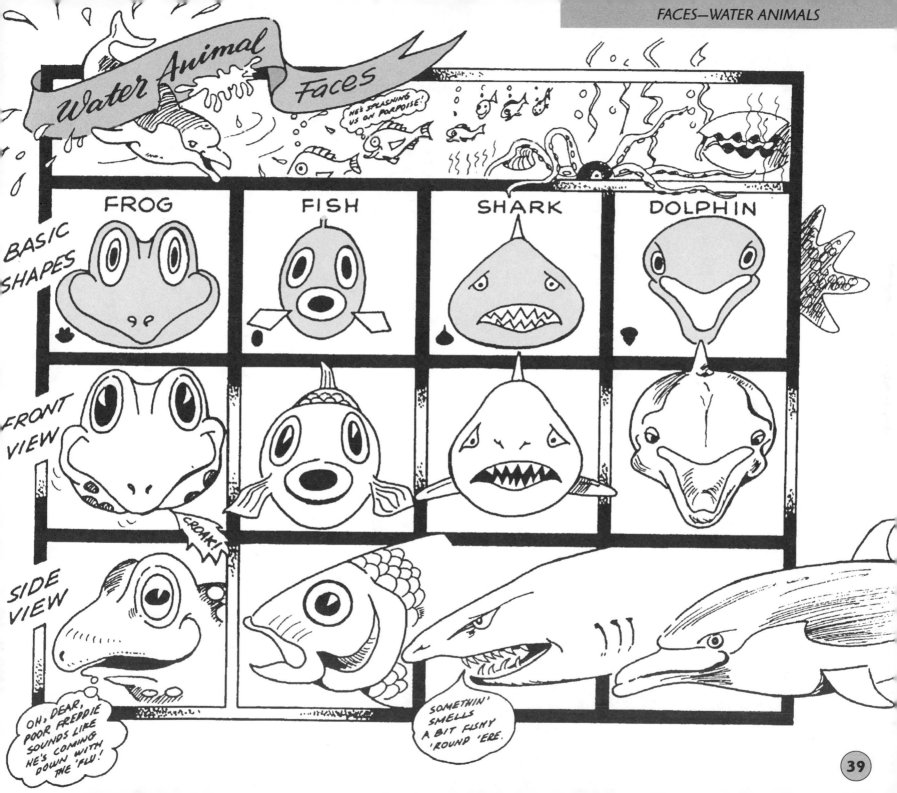

39

NOW... we'll attach BODIES to all the faces

CAT DOG HORSE COW SHEEP

GOAT PIG DONKEY RABBIT FOX

SQUIRREL MOUSE KANGAROO KOALA WOMBAT

PLATYPUS GIRAFFE ZEBRA CAMEL SPRINGBOK

MEOW!

RHINO   HIPPO   WART-HOG   ELEPHANT   TIGER

LION   LEOPARD   PANTHER   CHEETAH   JAGUAR

COUGAR   LYNX   MONKEY   CHIMPANZEE   GORILLA

BABOON   WOLF   HYENA   JACKAL   DINGO

BULL-TERRIER   ENGLISH SHEEPDOG   BLOODHOUND   POODLE   COLLIE

SNIFF SNIFF

More ANIMAL BODIES...

BULLDOG — SCOTTISH TERRIER — GERMAN SHEPHERD — BEAR — BISON

DEER — MOOSE — CHIPMUNK — RACCOON — SKUNK

BEAVER — LLAMA — TAPIR — ARMADILLO — ANTEATER

PANDA — YAK — WATER BUFFALO — DRAGON — BADGER

MOLE — WEASEL — HEDGEHOG — OTTER — FERRET

SHREW

VOLE

SEAL

WALRUS

PENGUIN

POLAR BEAR

HEN

DUCK

GOOSE

TURKEY

ROBIN

PARROT

OSTRICH

EMU

OWL

EAGLE

VULTURE

PELICAN

SNAKE

FRILL-NECKED LIZARD

TORTOISE

CROCODILE

FROG

FISH

SHARK & DOLPHIN

Don't forget to *exaggerate* their features
if you want to make them *more* cartoonish.
(See pages 44 - 47
for ideas.)

NOTE:

IN THE CATALOGUE PART OF THIS BOOK THAT YOU HAVE JUST LOOKED AT I HAVEN'T MADE THE ANIMALS LOOK <u>TOO</u> CARTOONISH.

I DID THIS BECAUSE IT'S VERY HELPFUL TO KNOW WHAT THE ANIMALS <u>REALLY</u> LOOK LIKE.

HOWEVER...

IF you want to make your animal faces *more* 'cartoonish' than I've drawn them, just use the catalogued drawings to give you the idea of the *features* and *basic* *shapes* — and then loosen-up your style a bit —

like this...

THE CATALOGUE DRAWING
(SEE PAGE 28)

The *more* 'cartoonish' rendition

Some *characteristics* of a *cartoon*...

EXAGGERATED FEATURES
(THE CURVE OF THE NOSE)

BIG POPPY EYES

HOW DO YOU DO?

VERBAL BUBBLE

SMILE OR HUMAN TYPE EXPRESSION

SKINNY NECK

LET'S...
LOOK MORE CLOSELY
AT WHAT HELPS MAKE UP A
CARTOON FACE

 **POPPY EYES**    **NORMAL EYES**

 BIG SMILE
(OR OTHER 'HUMAN' FACE EXPRESSIONS)  **NORMAL MOUTH**

 EXAGGERATED FEATURES  **NORMAL SNOUT & EARS**

 **SKINNY NECK**  **NORMAL NECK**

NOW DRAW ME A **BIG** CARTOON BONE!

 ← NORMAL BONE

46

Some more examples...

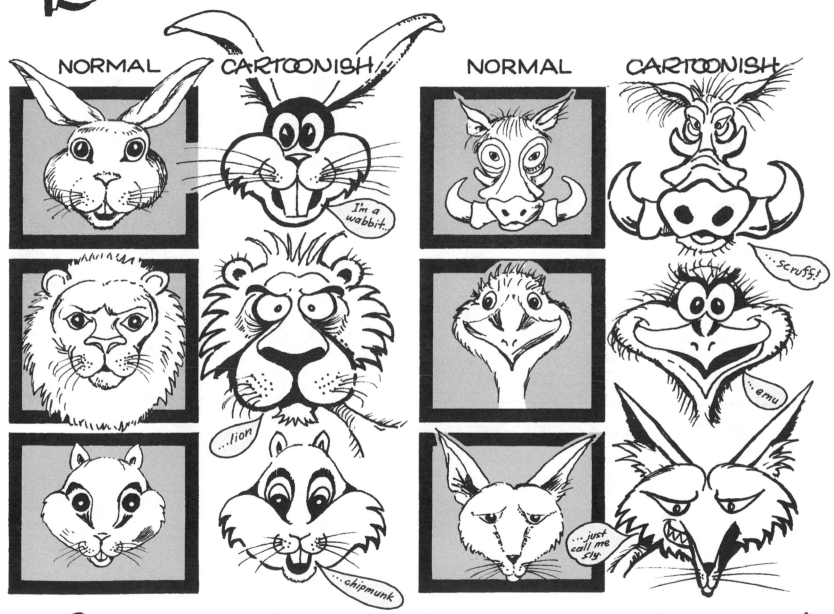

Once you know what the normal features of an animal are, try experimenting with your own exaggerations... It's FUN!

NOW... let's put some EXPRESSION into an animal's face.

WE'LL USE A RABBIT'S FACE.

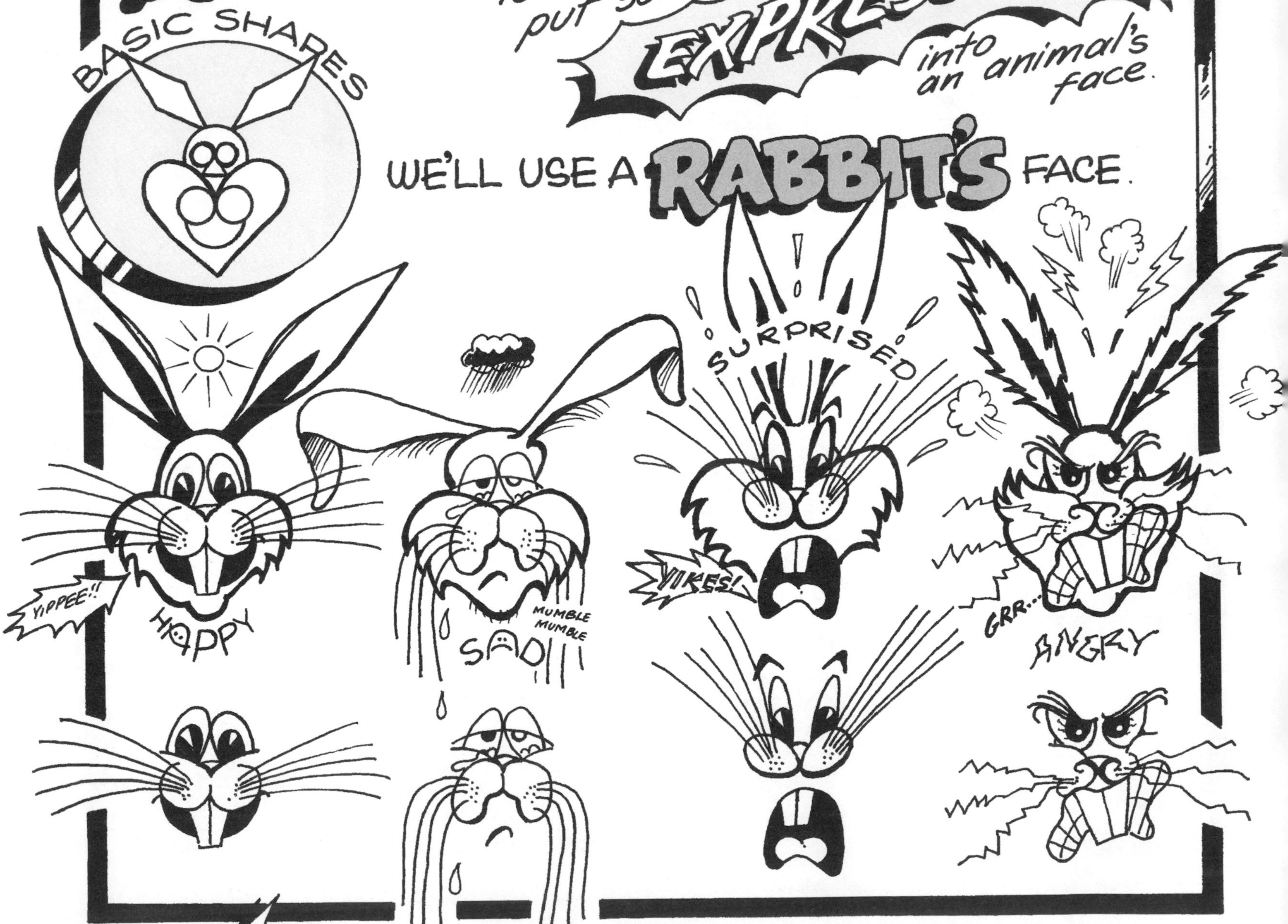

BASIC SHAPES

YIPPEE!!

HAPPY

SURPRISED

YIKES!

MUMBLE MUMBLE

SAD

GRR...

ANGRY

SEE HOW THE EYES AND MOUTH TELL A STORY!

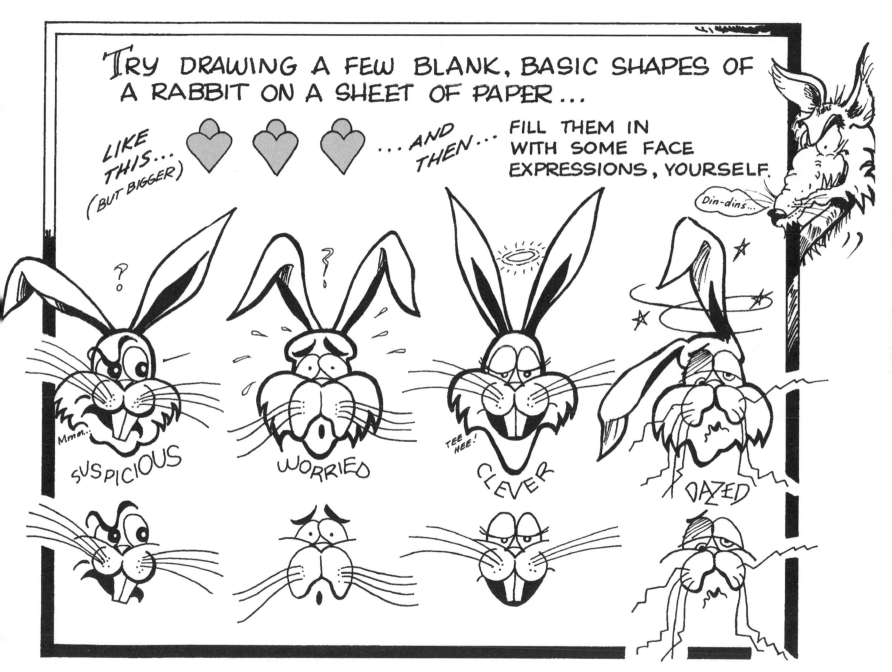

* NOTICE HOW EVEN THE EARS, CHEEKS AND WHISKERS CAN BE USED TO EXPRESS FEELINGS.

ANIMAL BODIES

CAN ALSO BE BROKEN UP INTO... SHAPES

I LIKE BIG, JUICY, ROUND SHAPES.

Always try to look for the shapes the body is made up of.

For example...

AN ELEPHANT

AN ELEPHANT'S SHAPES

I FEEL ALL BROKE UP!

ROUND IS BEAUTIFUL!

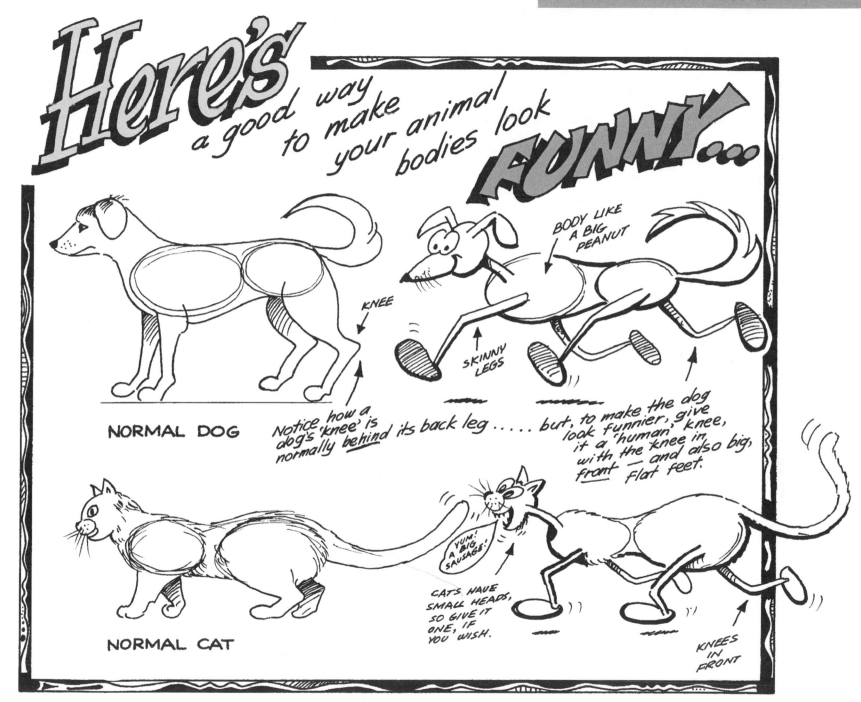

HERE *is an easy UPRIGHT body you can use for most animals...*

YOU CAN PUT QUITE A NUMBER OF DIFFERENT TYPES OF ANIMALS' HEADS ON THIS BODY.

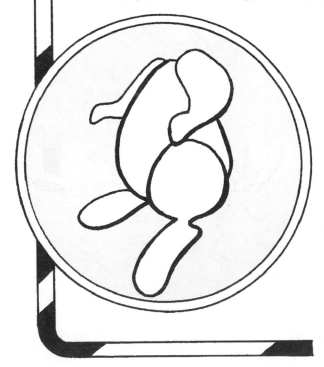

YOU USE THIS BODY ESPECIALLY FOR ANIMALS WHICH SOMETIMES STAND ON THEIR HIND LEGS. FOR EXAMPLE: RABBITS, MICE, RATS, CHIPMUNKS, BEARS, ETC...

...ESPECIALLY BABY ANIMALS.

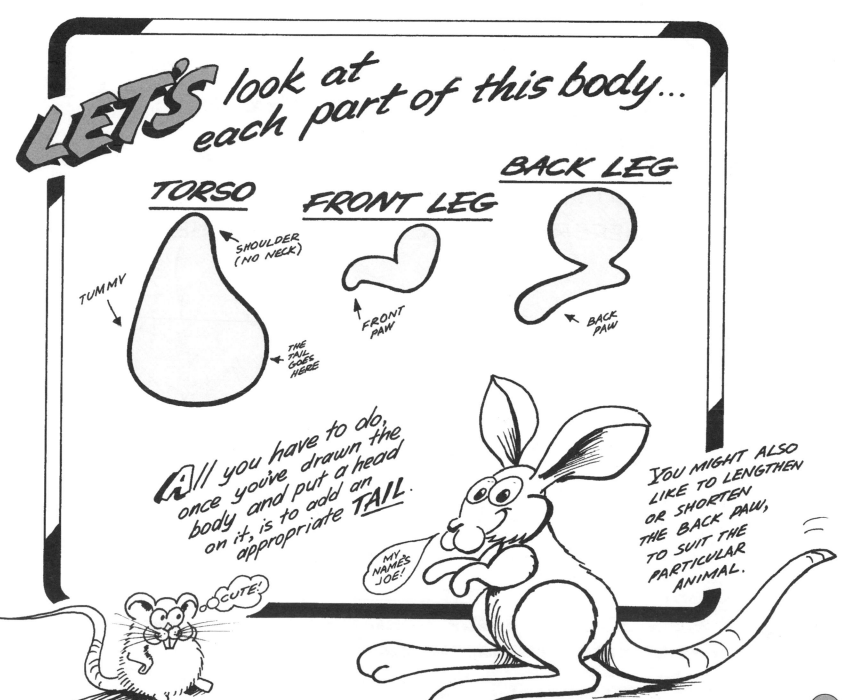

LET'S look at each part of this body...

TORSO

SHOULDER (NO NECK)

TUMMY

THE TAIL GOES HERE

FRONT LEG

FRONT PAW

BACK LEG

BACK PAW

All you have to do, once you've drawn the body and put a head on it, is to add an appropriate TAIL.

CUTE!

MY NAME'S JOE!

YOU MIGHT ALSO LIKE TO LENGTHEN OR SHORTEN THE BACK PAW, TO SUIT THE PARTICULAR ANIMAL.

Other **cute** animals...

BIG BRIGHT EYES

NO NECK

CUTE SMILE

FAT TUMMY

BABY ANIMALS HAVE BIG HEADS

YOU CAN MAKE THEM LOOK FLUFFY, TOO.

BIG PAWS

Keep them a bit chubby — without a neck... they look cuter that way.

NOTE...

I drew the cartoon characters on these two pages simply by looking at photos of the animals in a book and then <u>EXAGGERATING</u> their features...

... keeping in mind what features make up a *DORKY* character :

- SKINNY BODY
- SKINNY 'ARMS' & LEGS
- LARGE 'HANDS' & FEET
- KNOBBLY KNEES & ELBOWS
- HAIRY 'ARMS' & LEGS
- SKINNY NECK
- BULGING ADAM'S APPLE
- NO CHIN
- BIG NOSE OR BEAK
- STUPID GRIN
- OPEN MOUTH
- TONGUE POKING OUT
- CROOKED TEETH
- BENT WHISKERS
- SLEEPY EYES
- FLOPPY, BENT EARS
- HAIRY EARS
- SCRUFFY HAIR OR RUFFLED FEATHERS
- DROOPY BODY (STOOP)
- BAGGY CLOTHES
(IF YOU USE THEM)

BLERP!

HI, ENA!

YOU'RE LOOKIN' GOOD, BABE!

TRY making up your own.... ANIMAL JOKES

HA HA HO HO

GRRR

GROWL BARK! BARK! YAP YAP WOOF!

YEOW

15

I think she's the one who's never ridden a horse before.

Now look who's a pretty boy!

I'd like to hire a suit — I'm marrying a princess at midnight, tonight.

At last I've gotten that jolly lamb off my trail!

MY FAVOURITE LETTERS COME IN THE MAIL-BOX!

Here's a great lettering style you can use with your cartoons.

ABCDEFGHIJK
LMNOPQRSTU
VWXYZ!?

You can do it one-stroke, too...
ABCDEFGHIJKLM
NOPQRSTUVWXYZ

You can also put a SHADOW behind the letters ABCDEFG!

The letters always look best if they OVERLAP a bit...

OVERLAP

INDEX

(MENU)

ALLIGATOR	62	DONKEY	17, 40
ANTEATER	30, 42	DRAGON	31, 42
ARMADILLO	30, 42	DUCK	35, 43, 55
BABOON	24, 41	EAGLE	37, 43
BADGER	32, 42	ELEPHANT	21, 41, 50
BEAR	12, 28, 42, 55	EMU	10, 36, 43, 47
BEAVER	29, 42	ENGLISH SHEEPDOG	26, 41
BISON	28, 42	FERRET	33, 42
BLOODHOUND	26, 41	FISH	39, 43
BULLDOG	27, 42	FOX	18, 40, 47
BULL-TERRIER	26, 41	FRILL-NECKED LIZARD	38, 43
CAMEL	20, 40, 57	FROG	39, 43
CAT	6, 16, 17, 40, 51, 54	GERMAN SHEPHERD	27, 42
CHEETAH	23, 41	GIRAFFE	20, 40
CHIMPANZEE	9, 24, 41	GOAT	17, 40
CHIPMUNK	11, 29, 42, 47	GOOSE	35, 43
COLLIE	27, 41	GORILLA	24, 41
COUGAR	23, 41	HEDGEHOG	32, 42
COW	16, 40	HEN	35, 43
CROCODILE	38, 43	HIPPOPOTAMUS	21, 41
DEER	28, 42	HORSE	16, 40
DINGO	25, 41	HYENA	8, 25, 41, 57
DOG	13, 16, 40, 46, 51, 55	JACKAL	25, 41
DOLPHIN	39, 43	JAGUAR	23, 41

THAT'S THE END OF THE TALE, FOLKS!

KANGAROO	19, 40, 53, 55	ROBIN	36, 43
KOALA	19, 40	ROOSTER	56
LEOPARD	22, 41	SCOTTISH TERRIER	27, 42
LION	11, 22, 41, 47	SEAL	34, 43
LLAMA	30, 42	SHARK	39, 43
LYNX	23, 41	SHEEP	17, 40
MOLE	32, 42	SHREW	33, 43
MONKEY	24, 41	SKUNK	29, 42
MOOSE	28, 42, 45	SNAKE	38, 43, 63
MOUSE	10, 18, 40, 53, 54	SPRINGBOK	20, 40
OSTRICH	36, 43	SQUIRREL	18, 40, 54
OTTER	33, 42	TAPIR	30, 42
OWL	37, 43	TIGER	11, 15, 22, 41
PANDA	31, 42	TORTOISE	38, 43
PANTHER	22, 41	TURKEY	35, 43
PARROT	36, 43	VOLE	33, 43
PELICAN	37, 43	VULTURE	37, 43
PENGUIN	34, 43	WALRUS	34, 43
PIG	15, 17, 40, 55	WART-HOG	21, 41, 47, 57
PLATYPUS	19, 40	WATER BUFFALO	31, 42
POLAR BEAR	34, 43	WEASEL	32, 42
POODLE	26, 41	WOLF	25, 41, 49
RABBIT	11, 14, 18, 40, 47–49, 54–56	WOMBAT	19, 40
RACCOON	29, 42	YAK	31, 42
RHINOCEROS	21, 41	ZEBRA	20, 40, 63